Purple, orange, yellow and blue:
The colors of the sunrise:
The colors of you...

Emerging forth for the world to see;
I look up at you;
You shine down on me.

Basking in your warmth a beauty to behold;
Your rays ignite me and set afire my soul.
I stretch and reach forth to feel the heat of you.

My heart sweats; I am wet like the early morning dew.
The day unfolds and I contain you within my embrace;
reveling in the memory of your light lingering upon my face.

Your memory like you is so unforgettable and complete.
In the morning I will await,
our spiritual retreat.

@KMCARRINGTON

www.ingramcontent.com/pod-product-compliance
Lightning Source LLC
Chambersburg PA
CBHW051352280526
45784CB00007B/2927